THE COPY BOOK

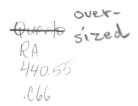
THE COPY BOOK

Copyright-free illustrations for development

donated by the Association of Illustrators
and other artists
introduced by BOB LINNEY and BRUCE WILSON

INTERMEDIATE TECHNOLOGY PUBLICATIONS   1988

ACKNOWLEDGEMENTS

The Copy Book was designed and laid out by Bob Linney. Great thanks are also due to the Association of Illustrators for its support and the use of its facilities, and particularly to Bruce Wilson. And then of course there are the illustrators, whose work *is* the book.

Thanks to: Meshack Asare, Helen Averley, Durga Baral, Rose Barnacle, Narenda Basnett, Janet Blakeley, David Bracken, Matt Brooker, Rachel Busch, Joanna Clutton, Jean Cozens, Terry Davies, Julie Douglas, John Erasmus, Jenny Fagence, Julia Foster, Teri Gower, Polly Harvey, Ron Hopkins, Elroy Hughes, Mary Jessop, Deepak Joshi, Ron Lumsden, Mohan Khadga, Jolyne Knox, Kim Leppard, George McBean, Chris Madden, Mike Munday, Sharad Ranjit, Elizabeth Rathmell, Jane Ray, Margaret Rollo, Ned Royal, Mike Sanderson, Joy Simpson, Jane Smith, Mark Urgent, Gini Wade, Jane Walton. Also thanks to Terry Aston of Ulster University and his student contributors: David Browne, Jim Carson, Carolyn Crory, George D'Arcy, Chris Esler, Karen Hunter, Sam Hunter, Kieran McClusky, Trevor McCormick, Wendy Robinson and Hugh Watt.

Published by Intermediate Technology Publications Ltd, 103–105 Southampton Row, London WC1B 4HH, UK.

ISBN 0 946688 44 3

Printed in England by The Short Run Press, Exeter

Contents

I. Introduction

1. Illustrations for development

In the poorest rural and urban areas of many underdeveloped countries there is a severe shortage of posters and visual aids for health and development.

As most fieldworkers know, it is a common and dispiriting experience to find only a solitary poster or teaching aid depicting a whole area of social concern. Regular visitors to health posts, for example, become immune to the messages on posters they have been seeing continually. And health workers, bored with the same old teaching aids, often discard them.

In addition, most of the visual material that is currently produced is not understood by poor, rural people because their level of visual literacy is low.

These two factors – the shortage of visual material and the low levels of visual literacy – are related. Because village people see very few pictures, their level of visual literacy is low. Because their level of visual literacy is low, it is often difficult to communicate with them through pictures.

The success of health and development programmes depends very heavily on communications. Simple visual materials are often the most appropriate means by which information can be disseminated. Effective use of such materials is usually essential, if poor communities are actually going to benefit from development programmes.

This book is an attempt to do something to help increase the amount of visual material produced in underdeveloped countries. As such, we hope it can provide a point of departure for field workers and local artists who want to make their own visual aids.

2. The aims of this book

We hope that this book will help, in an indirect way (i.e. through copying and by suggestion), to stimulate the increased production of visual materials at a local level. The book aims to encourage local workers to make their own drawings by copying and adapting the book's illustrations for their own use.

The contributing artists have agreed that the drawings in the book should be free of copyright restrictions. This means that any development worker is free to exploit the book, either as instant artwork or as source material that can be copied or adapted.

It does not cost a lot of money to be creative. Most of the money spent on information campaigns or materials production in underdeveloped countries goes into paper, printing and distribution costs. It is probably almost as cheap to re-design and improve materials as it is to reprint old designs, if local artists are given the responsibilities which their skills deserve.

Another aim has been to introduce British illustrators to development communications, as a possible alternative to their work in commercial advertising at home.

Pen and ink line drawings are particularly appropriate tools for visual communication because of the ease with which they can be reproduced. The simpler the drawing, the greater are the possibilities for reproducing it. Printing houses with even the most basic equipment can duplicate line drawings much more efficiently than they can photographs. At another level, it is cheap and relatively easy to copy line drawings by hand.

We also hope that the book will be used by schools as an aid in classes on art, development and health. Art teachers and students might wish to turn their attention to health and development issues. Schoolchildren can be encouraged to think that there might be a place for them in the profession of development communication, as governments and aid agencies begin to realize the importance of using artists in development programmes.

3. Limitations of the book

Many of the drawings in this book have been done in Britain. Because of this, they are not, as they stand, correct and fully relevant to local situations in the Poor World.

[vii]

Most of the drawings do not claim to be specifically relevant to any particular locality. However, we hope that, if the drawings are adapted carefully and sensitively, the book will help field workers to make useful visual aids in their own local situations.

It is, of course, possible to make country-specific versions of *The Copybook*. This has already happened in a few cases and we hope that this book will also encourage people to do the same in other countries.

II. How to Use this Book

We hope that you will use the illustrations in the book to help you draw figures and objects that you may need for making posters and other visual aids.

Please use the drawings FREELY. Although the illustrations cover a wide range of specified subjects, you can take whichever bits you want and put them to any purpose. Don't feel that you need to stick to the categories used here. Don't copy the drawings exactly, but change them so that they are appropriate for YOUR local situation – for example, draw LOCAL dress-style, LOCAL hair-styles and so on.

Sometimes you may want to trace a drawing directly from the book. At other times, you may need to enlarge one of the drawings for your own purposes. You may also want to use only parts of the pictures or to combine two or more pictures from the book to make your own visual aid. Some practical tips are given below, and these should help you to make full use of the drawings.

The field-testing or pre-testing of visual materials before they are mass-produced is an important way of maximizing the effectiveness of your designs. When you have made a rough draft of your design, show it to some of the people from the community you are working with. Ask them to tell you what the design means to them, and take a careful note of any criticisms they make. If people have problems in understanding your draft design, you should change the design before making multiple copies of it.

If you do succeed in making a visual aid with the help of this book, we hope you will be encouraged to make others. Remember that visual stimulation is as necessary in getting a message across as pre-testing. You can provide this kind of stimulation by producing more visual aids more often for the same subject area.

Furthermore, you should not feel that because basic development messages are 'good for people' they will automatically be absorbed and acted upon. There is no evidence to suggest that people respond more positively to messages urging them to adopt good or healthy practises. Try to monitor the useful-ness of any visual aids, and evaluate them as you use them in your work.

1. Some guidelines for designers

There are some simple guidelines which, if you follow them, will help you to make visual aids that communicate their messages well.

These guidelines were given to most of this book's contributors before they made their drawings. The guidelines should also be useful to any artist interested in development illustration, as well as to those who feel that they 'cannot draw', or who have had no previous experience of designing visual material.

The notes serve to highlight the fact that many non-literate people don't perceive and understand pictures easily.

○ Remember that your main concern is to make a design that shows objects or figures that can be RECOGNIZED by the community you are working with. Your design should be realistic and relevant. Try to include figures and objects that are FAMILIAR to the community.

○ It is usually best not to include any abstract symbols in your design. People do not always understand symbols like crosses, arrows or ticks, particularly if they are non-literate. The same is true of maps, diagrams and graphs. Most poor, rural people would have great difficulty in recognizing these kinds of visual symbols.

○ Many people find it difficult to understand pictures which try to show something moving. For example, if you show, in your design, a stream of water being poured from a pot, this may not be understood. People will not always understand that the 'water' in your drawing is meant to look as if it is moving. The same applies to things like the flames of a fire or ripples spreading across the surface of a pond. If you do need to try to show movement in your design, make sure during pre-testing that people understand that particular part of the design.

[ix]

○ Usually, pictures of people are easily recognized. Sometimes you will not want to show the whole body of a person (or people) in your design. This may be because there is not enough room on the paper to show whole figures. If so, be careful to show enough of the figure so that it is recognizable as such. If you only show a small or isolated part of a person's body in your design, difficulties may arise. For example, if you show only the head or hands of a person, the viewer may be confused.

○ It is best not to include too much detail in the background of a design. Do not include any background detail that is not strictly relevant to the main message of your visual aid. Irrelevant background detail plays no useful part in helping your design to communicate its message and it can often be distracting and confusing.

○ People and objects in your design should be drawn in the same proportions as they appear in everyday experience. If something is small in everyday life, it may not be recognized if it is drawn large on a visual aid. Similarly, something that is, in reality, large should not be drawn too small in your design.

○ Communication is often clearer if there is only a single centre of attention in your design. Try to make sure that this centre of attention (which might, for example, be a picture of a mother breastfeeding) is clearly separated from the background.

○ You may want to make a design in which there are a series of pictures that are meant to be read in a particular sequence. If so, remember that people will not always know that the different pictures are meant to be read in that sequence (or, indeed, in any sequence). Try, in some way, to make the correct reading sequence clear.

○ Many people will not be able, straight away, to understand cause and effect relationships between two objects, or elements, in your design. For example, if your design showed a picture of a healthy child, together with a picture of some nutritious food, people will not automatically understand the message that 'A child will be healthy if she eats nutritious food'. It is quite possible for people to RECOGNIZE the healthy child, and to RECOGNIZE the nutritious food, but not to associate the two things in a causal way.

○ Remember, lastly, that many people will not be able to understand extreme perspective or depth in a picture.

If you look at these guidelines again before you begin to sketch out a rough design for your visual aid, you will probably save yourself some time. The guidelines do not guarantee that your design will be effective, but they will give you a good starting point.

Because the guidelines are very general, it is possible that they will not all be relevant to your particular situation. Do not be unnecessarily restricted by them. Most important of all is to put pencil to paper and produce something, even if it is not perfect.

2. How to copy a drawing

In order to use this book to help make your own visual aids, you will need to be able to copy drawings from the book quite accurately.

Four different ways in which you can copy a drawing are outlined below.

(i) Imagine that you want to copy the drawing of a house shown on page 60.

This first method of copying is usually easy to do, even if you are not experienced at drawing.

First of all, draw horizontal lines across the picture in the book, using a sharp pencil and a straight edge, or ruler if you have one. Draw the lines so that they are an equal distance apart from one another.

Then draw a set of vertical lines across the picture in the book. The vertical lines should be drawn the same distance apart from each other, as are the horizontal lines.

This means that the picture in the book is covered by squares, as in the illustration below.

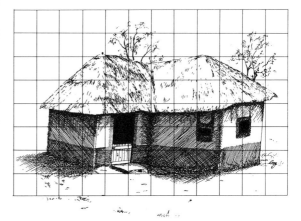

A set of horizontal and vertical lines drawn like this is called a 'grid'.

Next, take a sheet of paper, onto which you will make the copy of the drawing. Draw a grid of horizontal and vertical lines onto the plain sheet of paper. This grid should be the same size as the grid that you drew over the drawing in the book. That is, if you drew the lines in the book one centimetre apart from each other, draw them one centimetre apart on the new grid.

Now begin to copy the drawing onto the new grid. Look carefully in each square on the drawing in the book. Simply copy the lines in each square into the corresponding square on your new grid.

Look at only one square at a time and draw exactly what you see in that square. For example, you could begin with a square that contains in it the left-hand end of the house. When you have copied what is in this particular square, your copy would look like this.

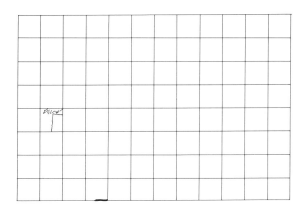

Then copy, one at a time, the squares next to the one you started with. Your copy might then look like this.

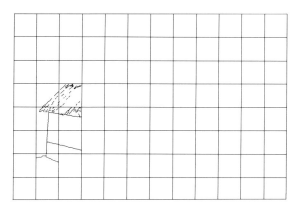

At this stage, you do not need to copy the shading on the walls of the house, for example. You can do this later. The important thing is to copy the MAIN LINES of the drawing.

When you have copied more of the squares, you will reach a stage where quite a lot of the main lines of the drawing are on your copy. For

example, the copy may look like this, at an intermediate stage.

Later, when you have copied all the main lines in the drawing, your copy will look something like this.

Lastly, you can add the shading to complete your copy.

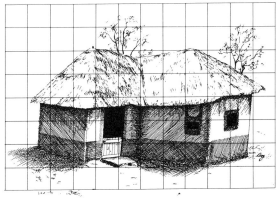

(ii) A second method of copying a drawing involves using 'tracing paper'. Tracing paper is thin paper that you can see through when you lay it over a drawing. It is not white in appearance, like ordinary paper, but greyish-white.

[xi]

So, if you can get a sheet of tracing paper, simply lay it over the drawing that you want to copy from the book. Using a pencil, draw over the main lines of the drawing, i.e. draw or trace the lines onto the tracing paper itself.

Then take a clean sheet of paper. Lay the tracing paper on top of the clean sheet UPSIDE DOWN, so that the pencil drawing on the tracing paper is in contact with the white paper.

Next, rub on the upper surface (i.e. onto the back of the surface that you drew on) of the tracing paper with the pencil. Rub or scribble on the tracing paper wherever there are lines on the drawing. This will press on the lines of the drawing and will transfer the lines onto the sheet of plain paper.

When you have scribbed over all the lines of the drawing, remove the tracing paper. A copy of the drawing will have been rubbed onto the white paper. You can now go over the lines on the white paper to improve your copy.

You will notice that, with this method, the copy you have made is back-to-front. That is, the copy is a reversal, or mirror-image, of the drawing in the book.

If you want to make a copy that is the same way round as the picture in the book, simply make a second copy of the first copy, using exactly the same method. When you copy the back-to-front copy, you will produce a second copy that is the same way round as the drawing in the book.

(iii) There is a third method of copying which also uses tracing paper. As in method (ii), again make a tracing of the drawing that you want to copy.

Place the tracing paper (with the main lines of the drawing copied onto it) over a new sheet of white paper. This time, the tracing paper should NOT be turned upside down. That is, the pencil drawing on the tracing paper should face upwards, so that it looks the same way round as the drawing in the book.

Then take your pencil and draw again over the lines on the tracing paper. This time, press as hard as you can without breaking the pencil or tearing the tracing paper.

By pressing hard you will make an outline on the white paper underneath. Remove the tracing paper and look carefully for the outline, which should be indented (or pressed) into the white paper. You will then need to draw over this outline with your pencil to produce the copy.

(iv) Lastly, you can, of course, make a copy of one of the drawings in the book if you have access to a photocopying machine.

3. *How to enlarge a drawing*

To enlarge one of the drawings in the book, you again need to draw a grid of horizontal and vertical lines over the drawing, as in the first method of copying described earlier.

When you have drawn this grid over the drawing in the book take a large sheet of plain paper on which to make the larger copy. You now need to draw another grid on the large sheet of paper.

The new grid should be larger than the grid you have drawn over the drawing in the book. If you want to enlarge the drawing so that your copy is twice as big as the drawing in the book, you need to draw the grid on the sheet of paper twice as large as the grid on the drawing. If you want to make a copy that is three times as big as the drawing in the book, draw a grid on the large sheet of paper that is three times as big as the one you drew over the drawing in the book—and so on.

Imagine, for example, that you wanted to make a larger drawing of the boy washing himself in the centre of page 31.

First of all, you would draw a grid in pencil over the drawing on page 31. If you have a ruler, a convenient size for the grid would be to make each of the horizontal, and each of the vertical lines, 5 millimetres apart.

To make a copy twice as big, you would need to draw a grid on the plain sheet of paper in which all the lines were two centimetres apart, like the one below.

Now you simply copy what is in each of the smaller squares over the drawing on page 31 into the corresponding squares on the larger grid. (This is exactly what you do when you make a same-size copy, as described earlier, except that you draw larger lines).

Go through the drawing, transferring it, square by square, onto the larger grid. One of the stages in the enlargement would look something like this.

Carry on copying what is in each square, one square at a time, until you have a drawing like the one numbered (4) which is twice as large as the first one.

Later you can remove the grid by rubbing it out with a rubber (eraser).

(1) First draw a grid 5 millimetres square over the original drawing.

(3) Copy the smaller picture, square by square, to the larger grid.

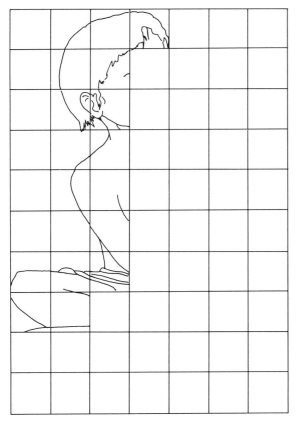

(2) Draw a grid twice the size, with squares of 10 millimetres (1 centimetre).

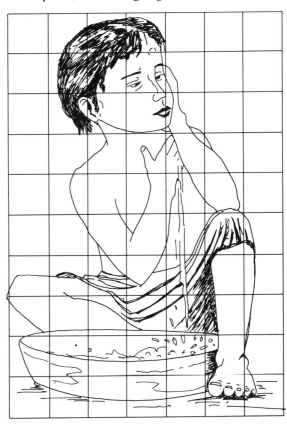

(4) Eventually the drawing is completed, twice the size.

4. How to adapt a drawing

You may find that you need to change or adapt the drawings in the book to suit your own purposes. That is, instead of copying or enlarging a drawing from the book exactly as it stands, you may want to change the drawing in some way so that it is more relevant to your needs.

This might involve changing the faces and/or hair-styles of the figures in the book. It might mean drawing different clothes on a figure so that the figure looks more like a person from the community you are working with. You might also want to change the position of an arm or leg, for example, on one of the figures drawn in the book.

There are so many different ways in which you might want to adapt the drawings that it is not possible to describe them all. We do hope, though, that you will use the drawings freely and not feel that you have to copy them exactly as they stand.

To illustrate two ways in which you could adapt the drawing of the boy washing, look at the illustrations below.

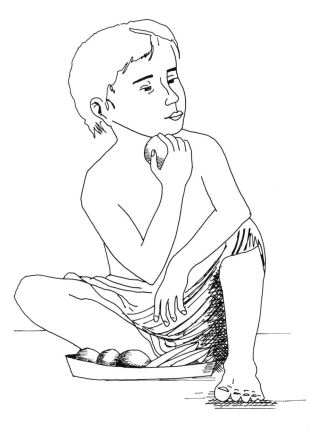

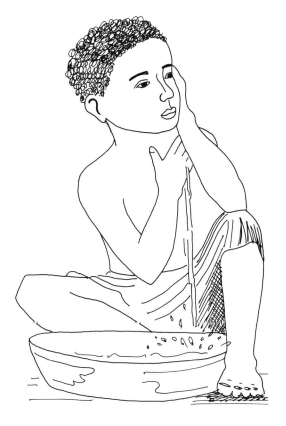

On the left, the boy's hair-style has been modified, while, above, the position of his arm has been changed so that he looks as if he is eating. The bowl of water has been changed into a dish containing food.

5. How to use part of a drawing

Another way you might want to use the book is to copy just one part of one of the drawings.

For example, instead of copying an entire figure from the book, you may want to show only the head and shoulders, on a larger scale. In that case, you need only to draw a grid over the head and shoulders of the figure in the book. You would then simply enlarge the head and shoulders onto a large grid drawn on the large sheet of paper on which you are making your design.

Thus, the drawing below could be used to make a new design. The head and upper part of the woman's body have simply been enlarged from the drawing on page 70.

[xiv]

The illustration below is an example of a design produced by combining some of the drawings used to illustrate earlier points.

You can also use just one figure from a drawing in the book that contains two or more figures. For example, the woman with the water pot from the drawing on the right can be taken and used on her own, as below.

6. How to combine different drawings

Lastly, it is, of course, possible to combine different elements from different pictures in the book, to make your own design.

Again, there are so many possible ways in which you could do this that we cannot describe, or even envisage, all of them. If you use the book freely and in a flexible way, and if you are prepared to adapt the drawings, you will find many possibilities for your own designs.

7. Lettering

Even though you will often be working with people who cannot read very well, you will often want to include some words in your designs.

Generally, it is best to use only a few words in the design, for simplicity and clarity. For example, it is usually said that a poster should have a main headline, often written above the pictures on the design, and consisting of six words or less.

If you do use words on your design, make sure that they are words which are understood by people in your community. Use simple, everyday words that are familiar to your audience, rather than longer, difficult, unfamiliar words whose meaning may not be easily understood.

When you come to draw the letters of the words on your design, you may want to use a straight edge to draw horizontal guidelines. But it is not necessary to make all the letters by using the straight edge. Drawing letters very carefully with a ruler takes a lot of time and, unless you do it perfectly, does not look particularly attractive.

It is a good idea to practise drawing simple letters free-hand. For the purposes of making visual aids for health and development work, you need only to learn how to make clear, bold, simple letters. For reference, we have shown on the next page a free-hand Roman alphabet (with apologies to people who may need to use other scripts).

ABCDEFG
HIJKLMN
OPQRSTU
VWXYZ
123456
78910

When you write the words on your design, be careful how you space the letters. Words should not be too spaced out, nor too squashed together.

You will probably find it helpful to sketch the words lightly across your design before starting to draw bold letters. For example, if you wanted to write 'Men Should Also Collect Water', you might start like this.

MEN SHOULD ALSO
COLLECT WATER

Just sketch the words lightly *in pencil* at this stage, to give yourself an idea of how the lettering fits across the page.

Then you may want to move some of the letters or words to the left or right. Do this by rubbing out the letters with an eraser and then sketch them in again in the correct positions.

Be careful not to leave large gaps between the letters of the same word. Try to keep the gaps between letters of the same word the same (i.e. equally spaced). Also, make sure that there are big enough gaps between different words so that they are clear and easy to read. These general principles about single lettering apply equally to sequences of pictures, and strip cartoons etc.

For example,

S HOU L D

does not look good because there are different sized gaps between the letters.

SHOULD

looks better, as the gaps are more equal.

MEN SHOULD ALSO

is not as easy to read as

MEN SHOULD ALSO

It is best NOT to try to do complicated lettering. It will take more time and will usually not be easy to read. If you concentrate on practising bold, clear, free-hand lettering, you will soon be able to make useful visual aids with clear, understandable verbal messages.

MEN SHOULD ALSO
COLLECT WATER

III. History

In 1984 George McBean, a communications officer with UNICEF in Nepal, wrote an article for the British Association of Illustrators' magazine, *Illustrators*, challenging commercial illustrators in the developed world to wake up to the harmful exploitation of their art by giant companies advertising drugs, junk food, etc., to the Third World. These illustrators, and the creative teams they worked with, should, George suggested, put their powerful marketing techniques into getting across more helpful messages. Field workers trying to persuade people in the Third World to adopt good health, hygiene and nutritional practices, for example, suffered from a terrible shortage of visual communication material: they stood little chance against the might of corporations peddling expensive, irrelevant potions.

In the following issue of *Illustrators*, readers wrote in supporting George's ideas. They were excited, but they also disputed the practicality of his call to action, and when George returned to London a forum was held where illustrators and designers, publishers and aid agency workers got extremely heated – George was now suggesting British illustrators put together a book of copyright-free visual material for the use of field workers, and this offended those professionals who were jealous of their monopoly on truth in development projects. How could these illustrators, these amateurs, possibly cope with the problems of visual literacy for example?

At this point Bob Linney, a British artist and designer with more experience in development communications than most, spoke up. The professional doubters were committing a bigger sin in preventing action than in allowing imperfect action to go ahead, he said. There was a crying need for visual material, any visual material, out there in the field, and the best thing we could all do was to stop arguing and get drawing. The audience broke into applause and as they filed out a significant number of illustrators volunteered to do drawings on development themes for George's book.

After the meeting, over a drink, George, Bob and the editor of *Illustrators*, Bruce Wilson, put together the outline of briefs to send to illustrators. Although some have dropped out since that day, many of these illustrators have been true to their immediate enthusiasm and have sent in drawings, and many new illustrators have joined in. And artists from countries as far apart as Sweden, Sierra Leone and Nepal have expanded the book beyond its original British cast of contributors.

A bundle of the first drawings, with an introduction written by Bob and George, was shown to Neal Burton at Intermediate Technology Publications. He liked the idea, floated it to colleagues, gave us excellent advice and, best of all, agreed to publish the book if we could promise enough drawings of the right kind.

Putting this book together has been a struggle, though not with the indolent consciences of British media folk. The difficulty has been to convince successful creative people that design and marketing for development campaigns can even exist as an area of commercial work worthy of attention. They will dig into their pockets for famine relief campaigns but they can't see that the work they do every day could be relevant to long-term development projects.

This book is one of the first stirrings of a new attitude and a new genre of design and illustration in the developed world. We hope it will inspire imitators, especially those making up for the deficiencies of this one; building on the experience of using it. During the three years it has taken to compile this book, Bob Linney's visual aid workshops, which he conducts on several continents, have grown into a new organization, Health Images, devoted to educating and encouraging media trainees in the developed world to take up designing and illustrating for development programmes. This and the welcome given to the idea of *The Copy Book* by Intermediate Technology Publications can be seen, we hope, as a sign of a much overdue input into the crucial yet neglected development area of getting the messages across.

Bruce Wilson
June 1988

FOOD

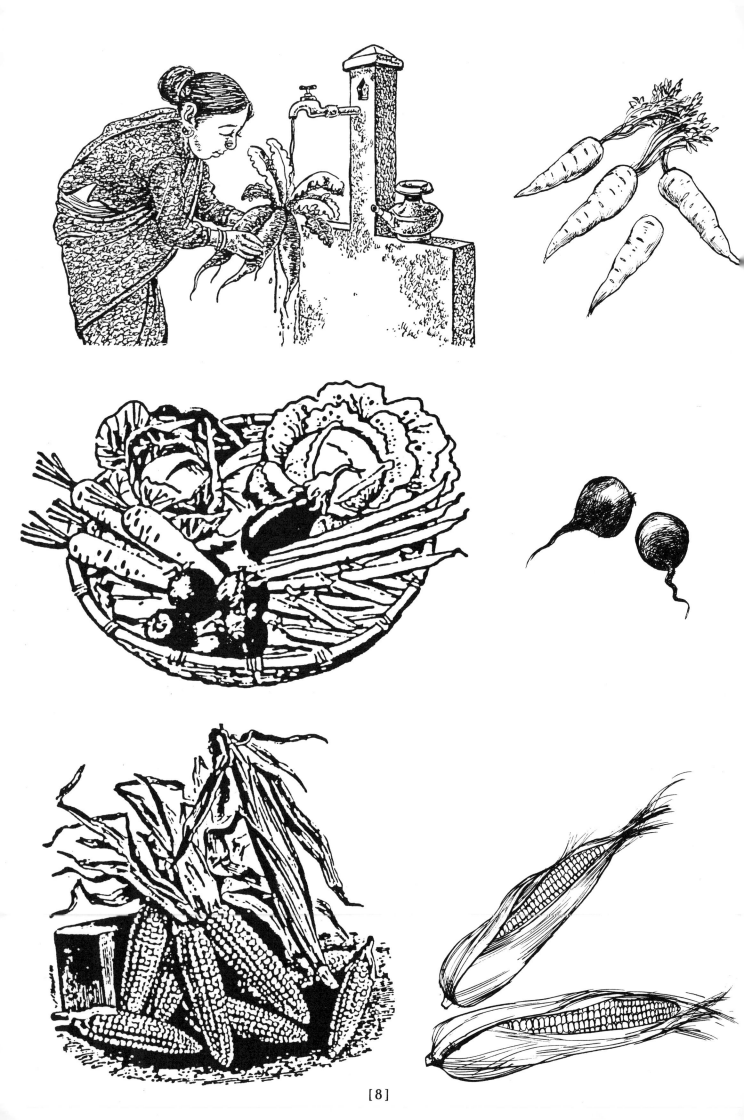

[8]

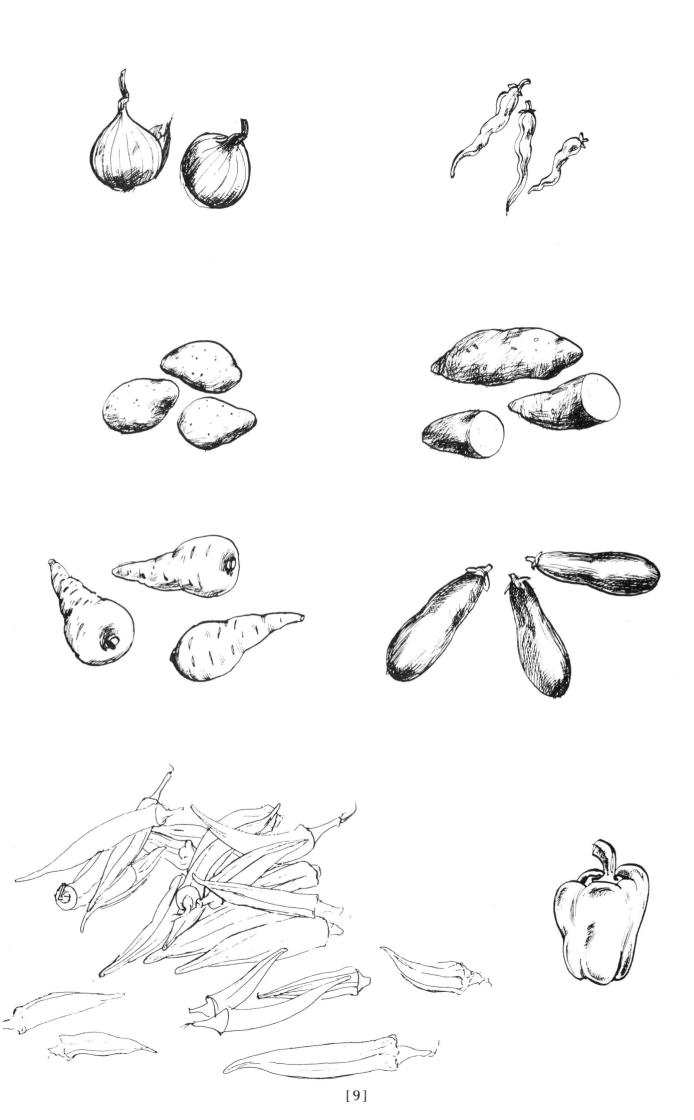

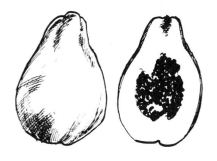

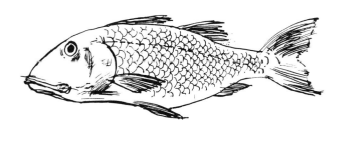

WATER AND HEALTH

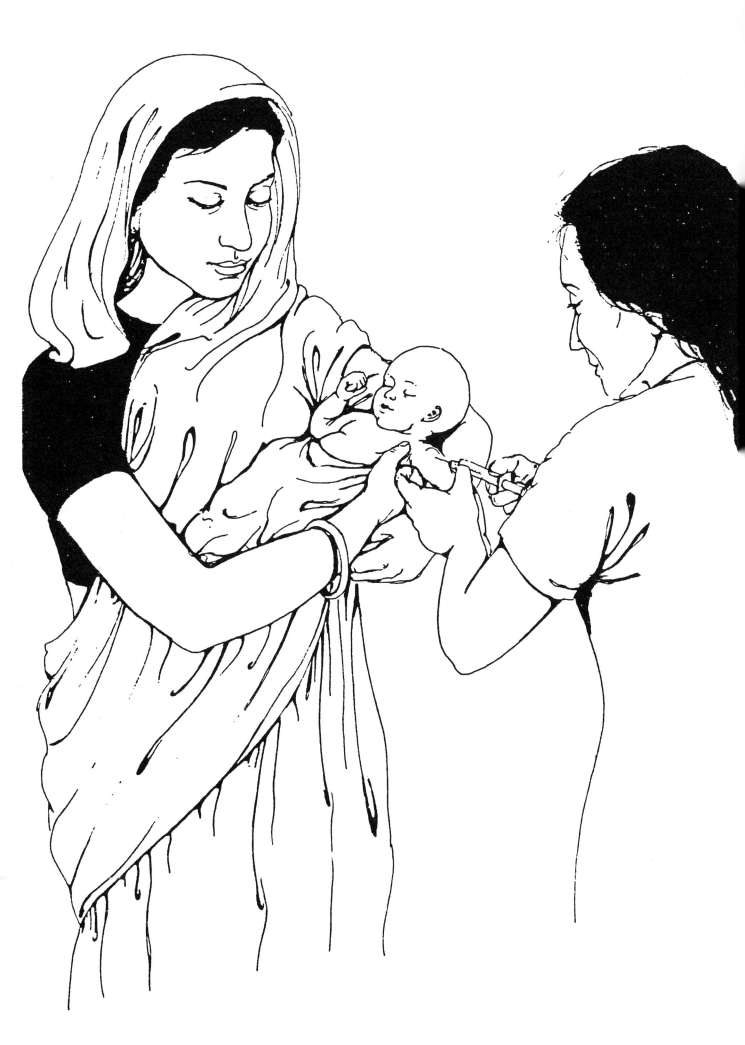

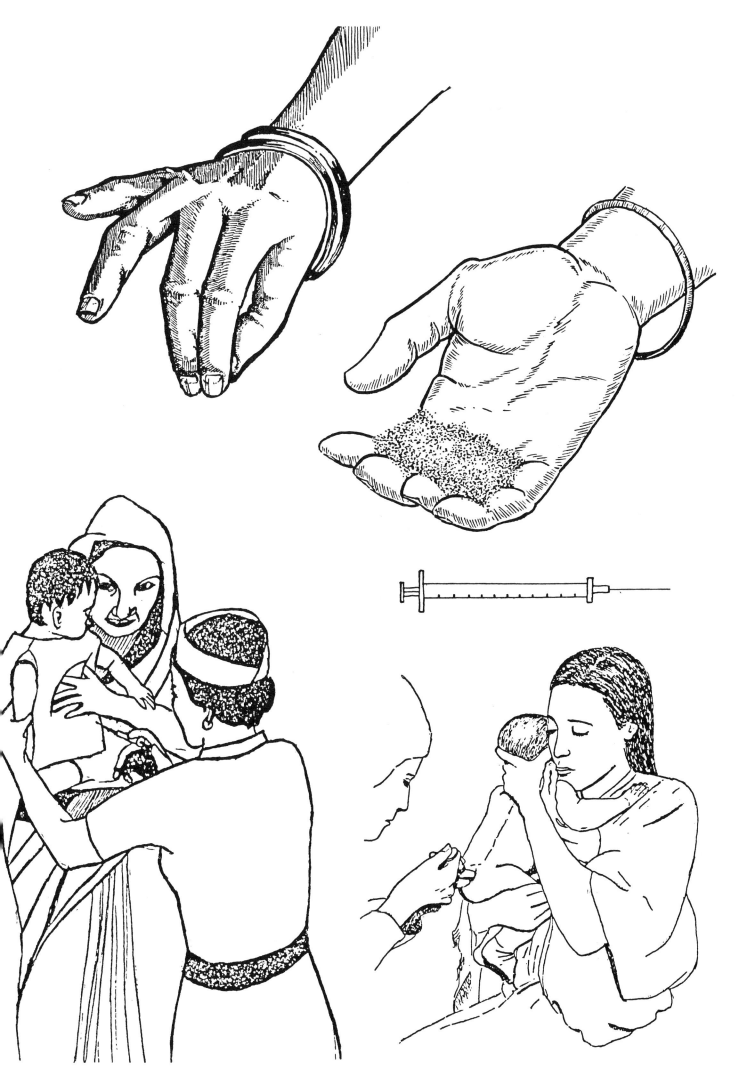

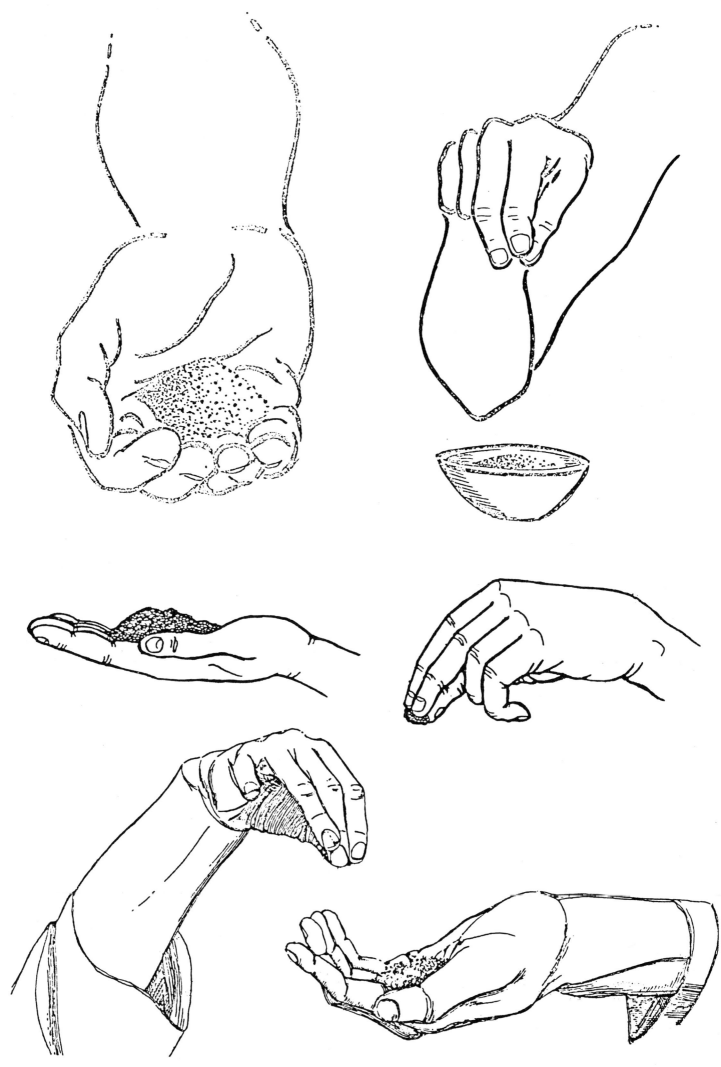

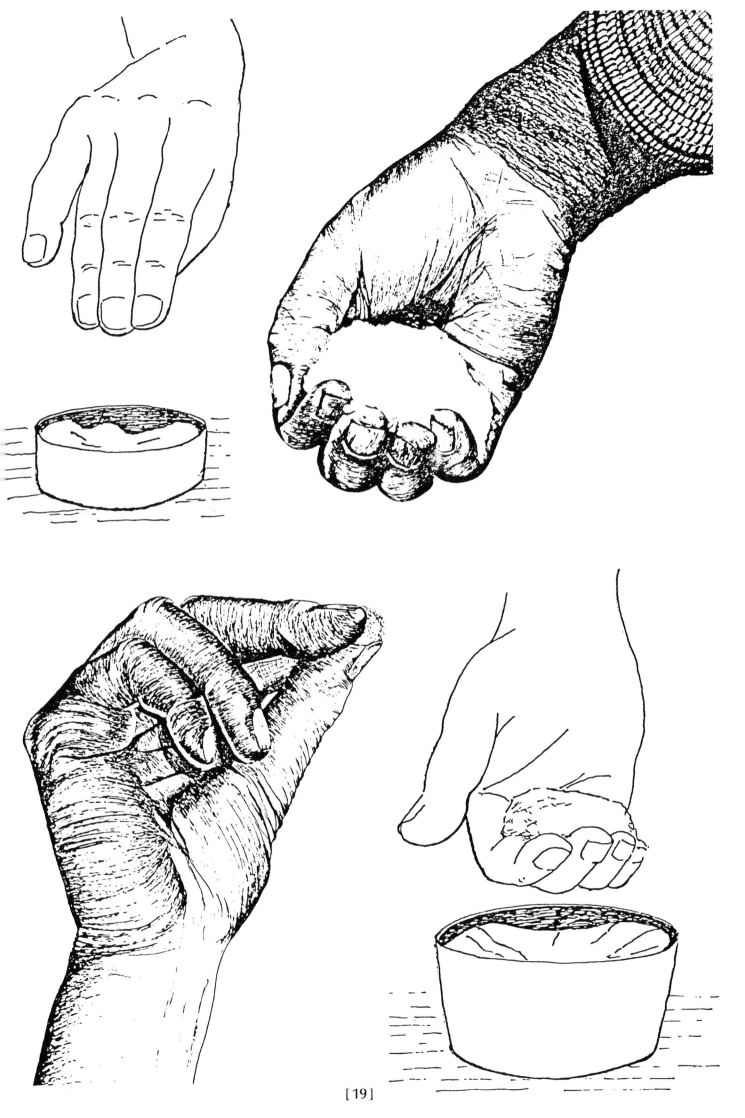

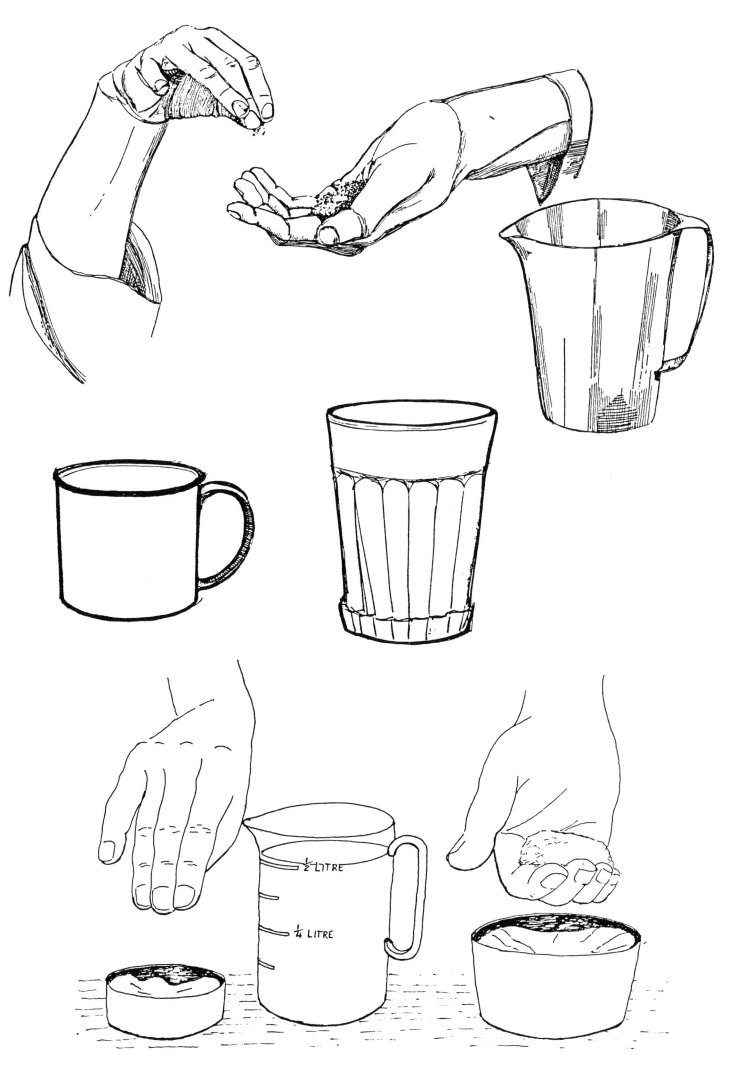

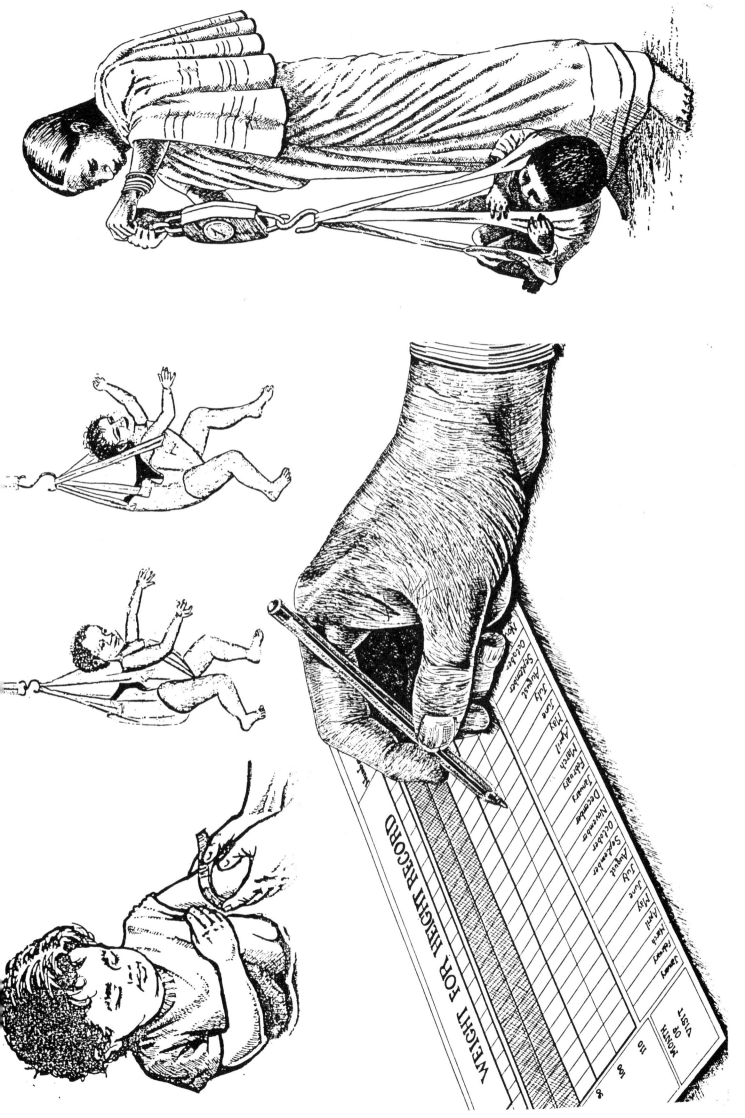

WEIGHT FOR HEIGHT RECORD

MONTH OR VISIT	January	February	March	April	May	June	July	August	September	October	November	December	January	February	March	April	May	June	July	August	September	October	November

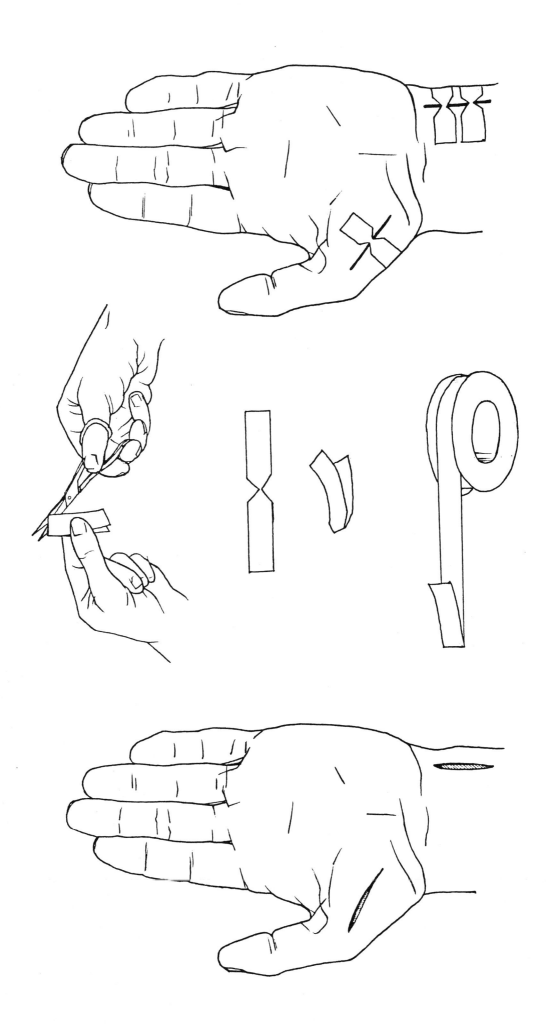

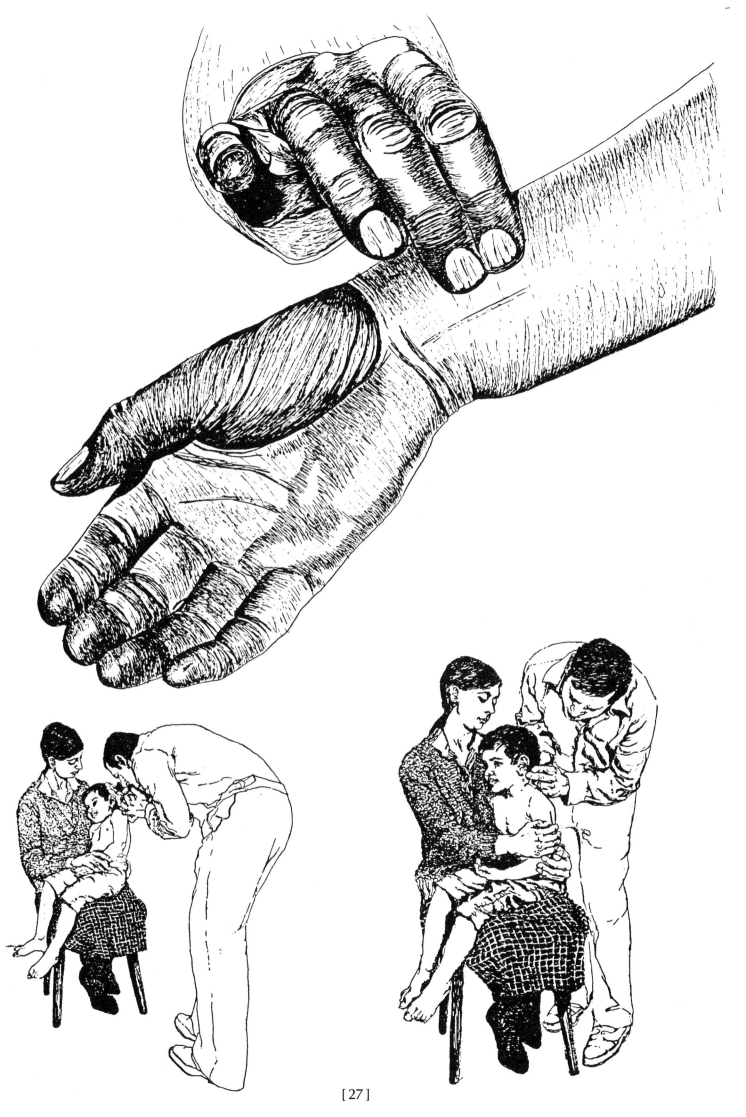

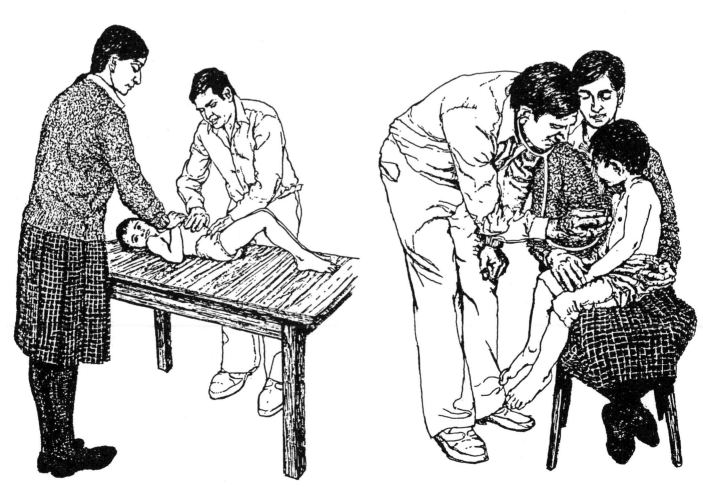

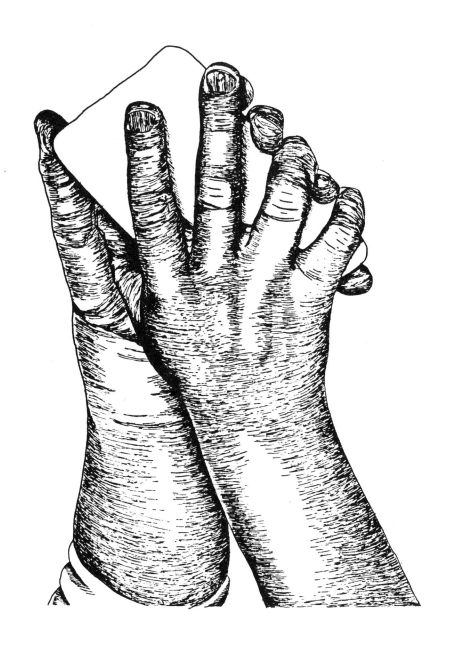

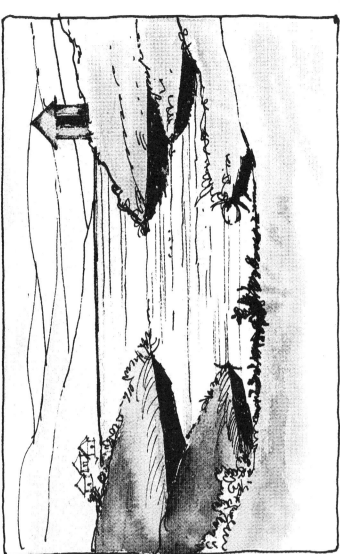

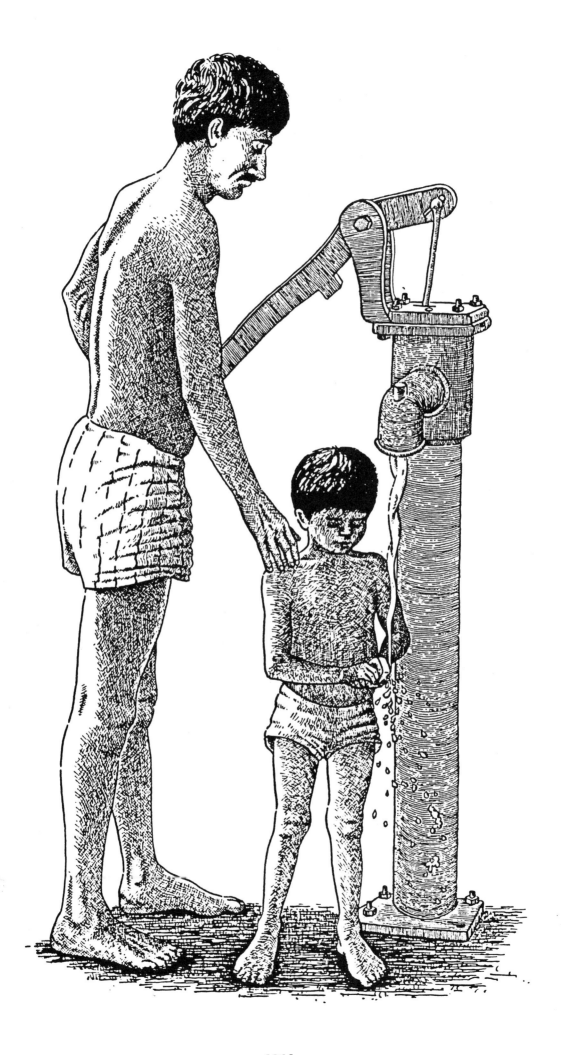

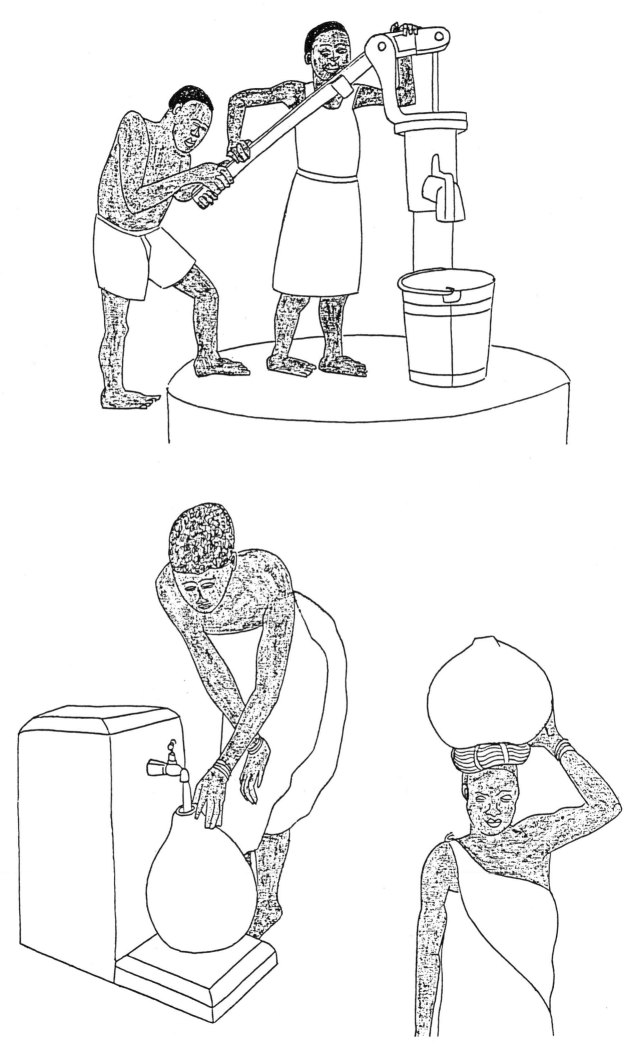

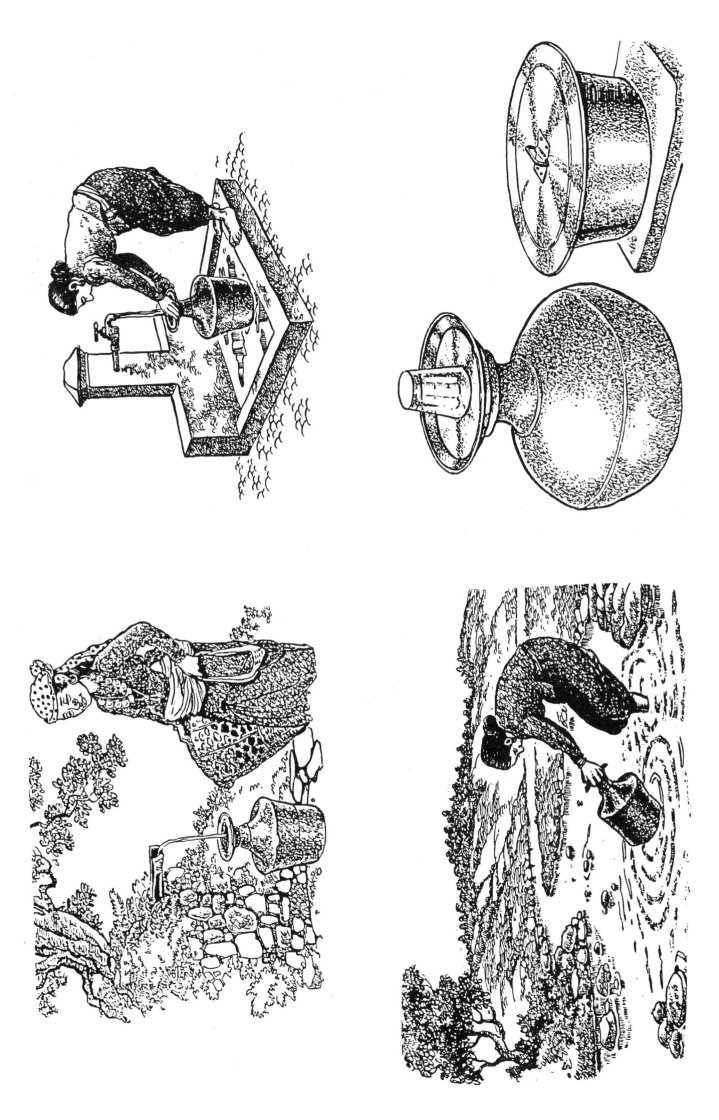

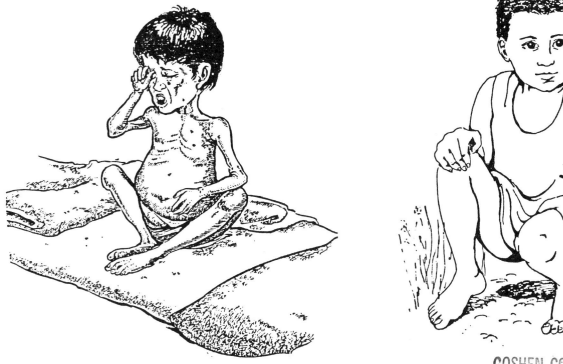

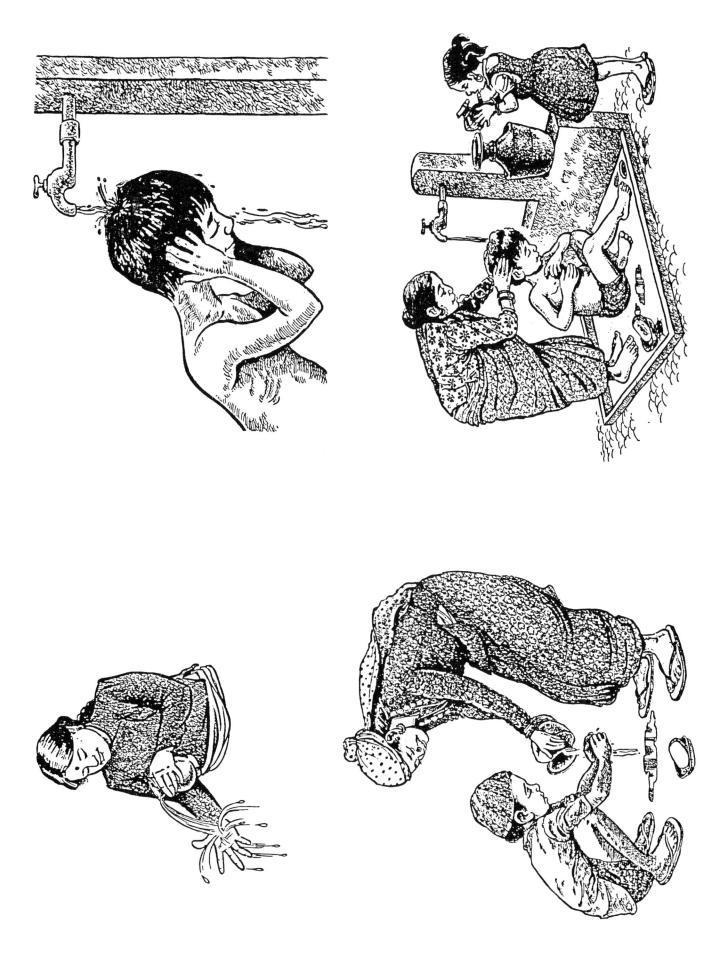

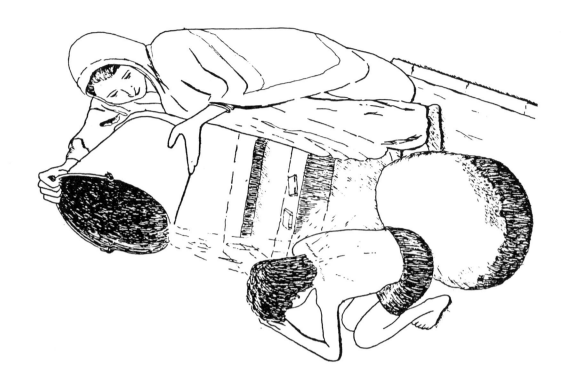

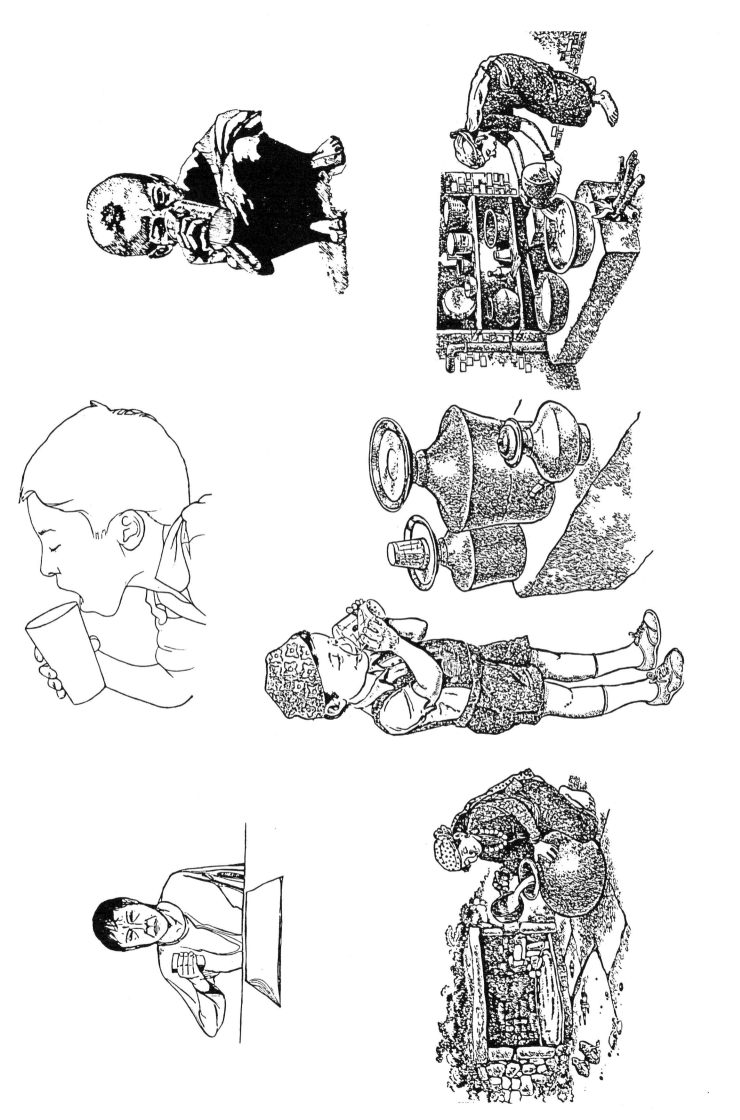

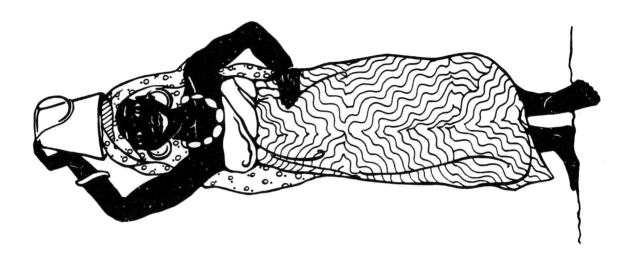
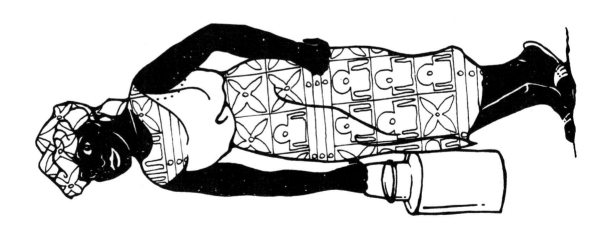

SHELTER

WORK

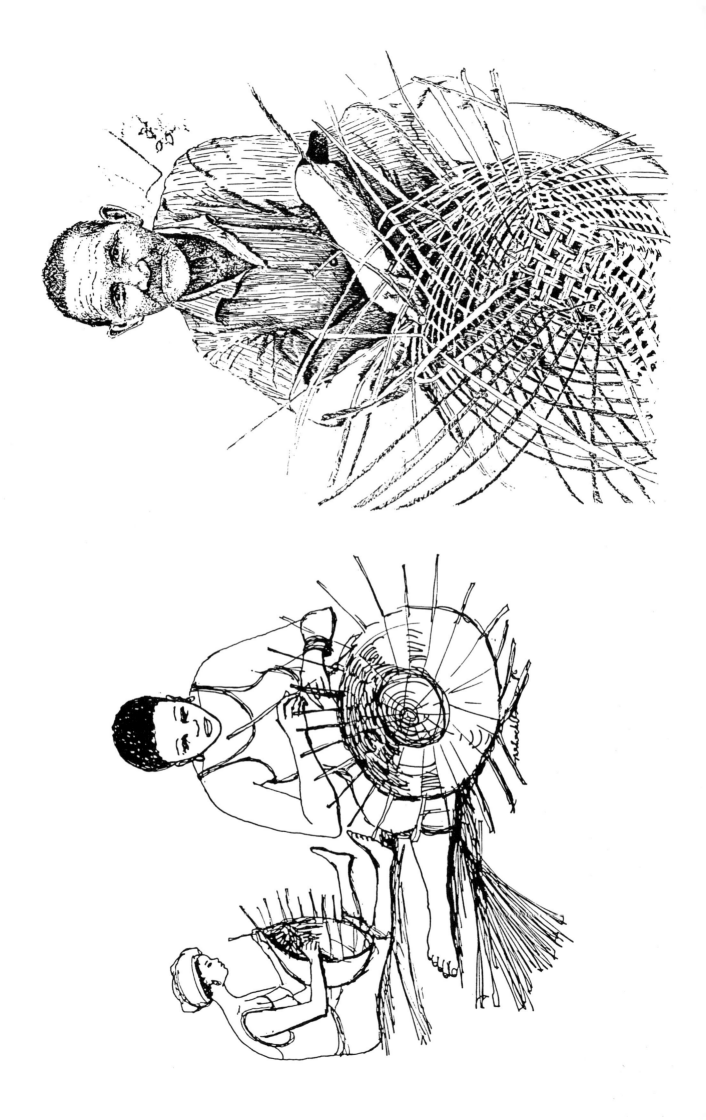

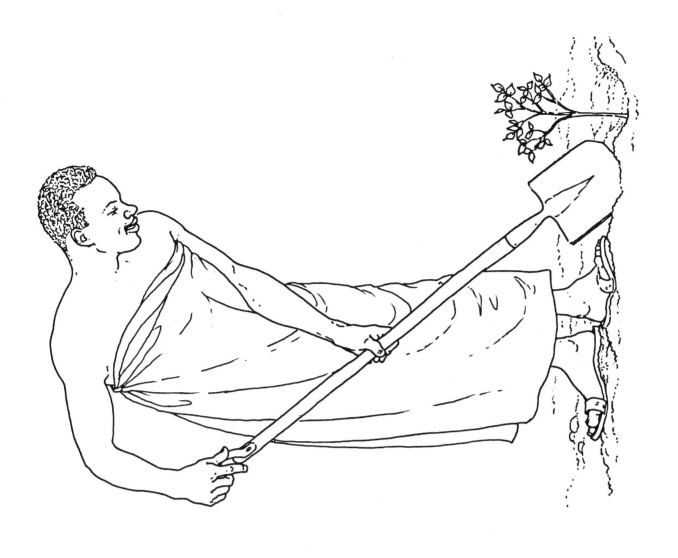

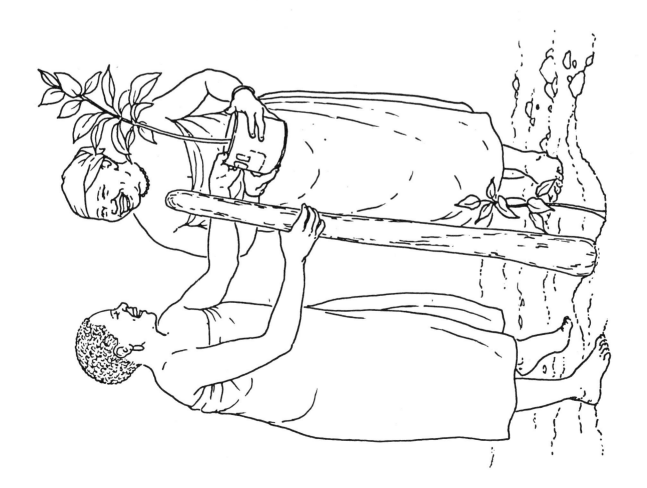

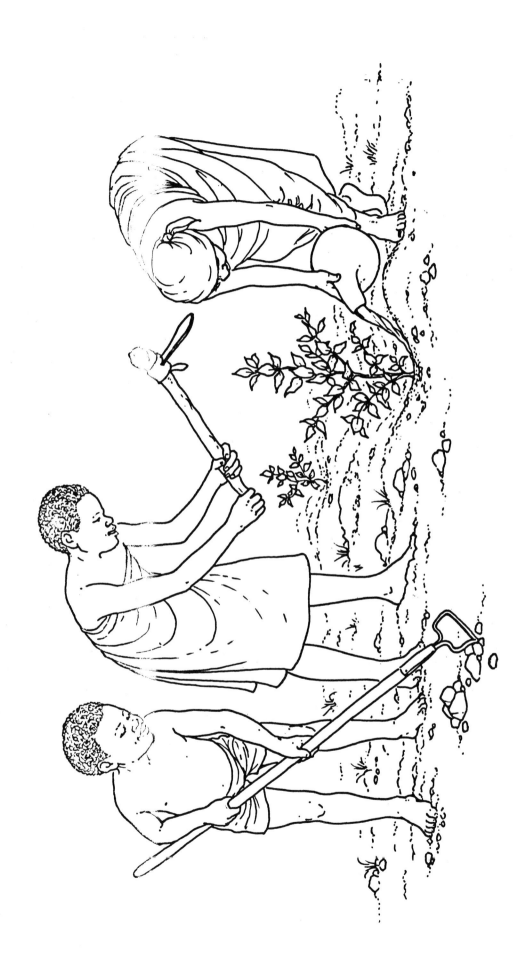

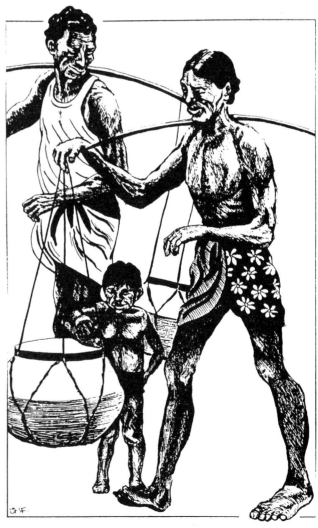

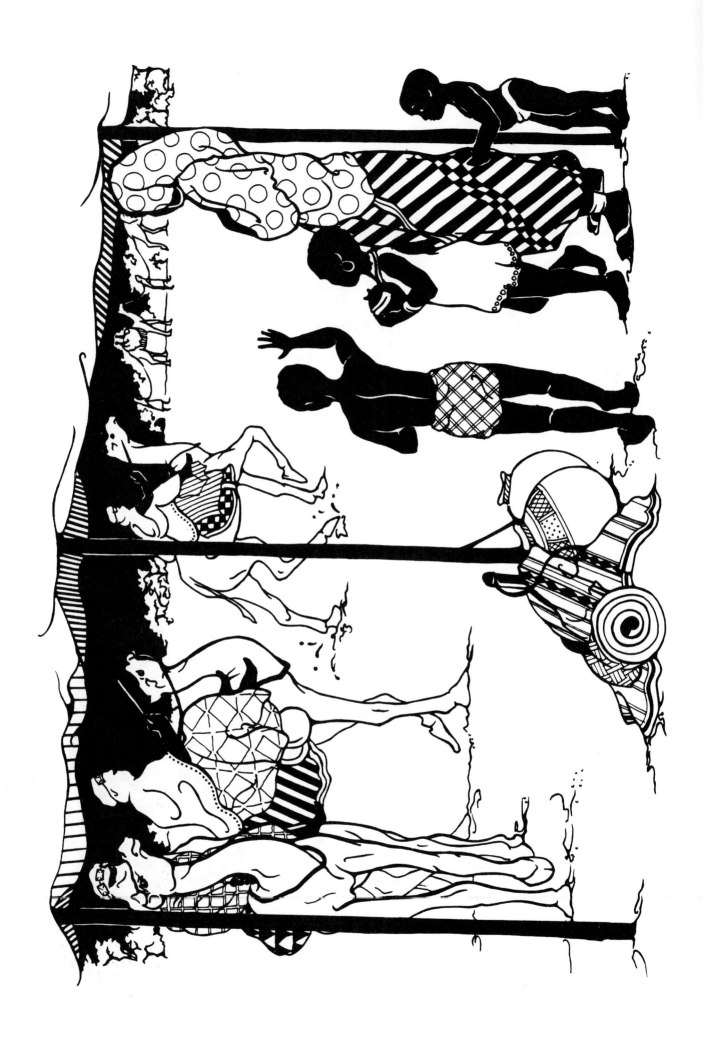

FIGURES, GROUPS AND COMICS

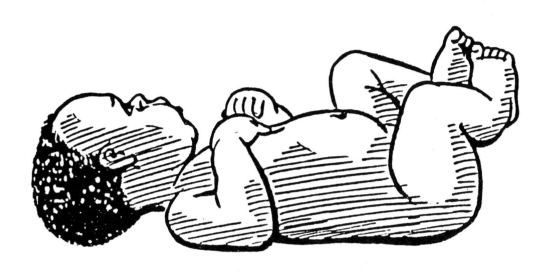

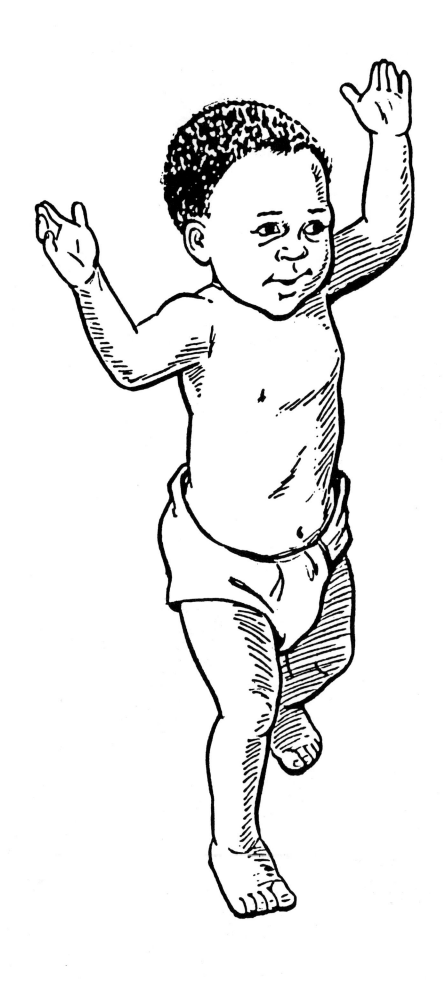

1

A pencil was used to make a rough drawing

2

A fine brush and ink were used to strengthen some of the lines and to put more details on the pencilled drawing. (keep only the best lines) The lines made in pencil were then rubbed off.

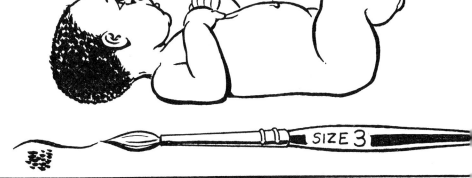

SIZE 3

3

Shading with a pen was used to show roundness and tone. Any writing pen that makes fine lines may be used.

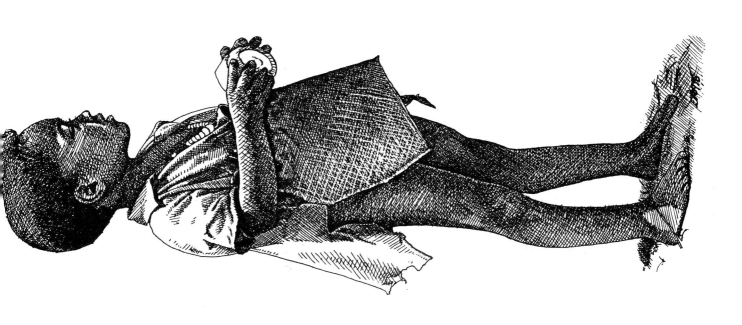

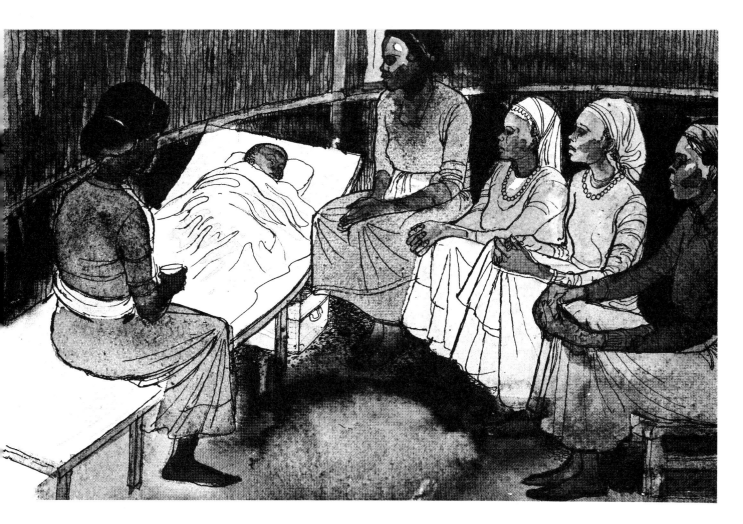

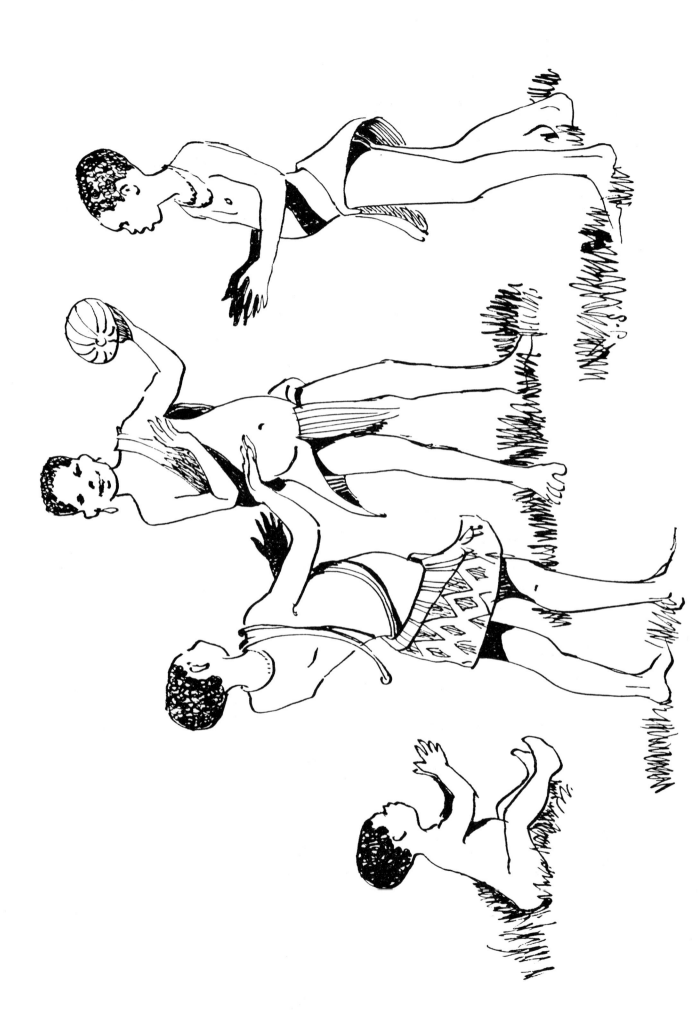

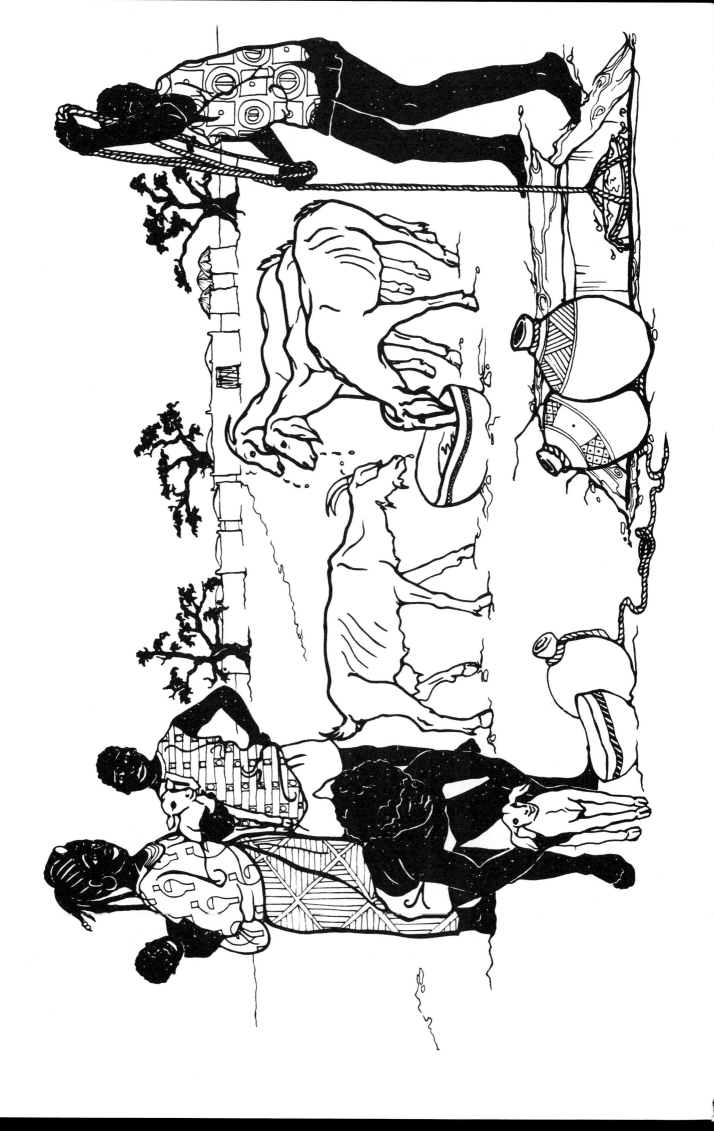

Oral ehydration Solution.

Water ½ litre

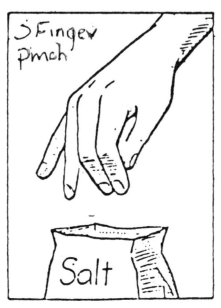

Salt

Scoop

Sugar

अक्कलेको अक्कल

SO IT WENT ON,

THE MORNING PASSED.

IT HAD ALWAYS BEEN LIKE THIS,

WORKING IN THE PLANTATION,

AND SO IT WOULD GO ON, NO DOUBT,

UNTIL SHE GOT MARRIED

AND HAD CHILDREN OF HER OWN

THEN BACK TO WORK IN THE PLANTATION

JUST LIKE HER MOTHER DID — AND HER GRANDMOTHER.* MEENA DIDN'T HAVE TO THINK OF ANY THING ELSE — WHAT GOOD WAS SCHOOL TO HER? SHE ALREADY KNEW HER FUTURE, A PLANTATION WORKER THAT'S WHAT SHE WAS, SO HOW COULD SHE CHANGE IT?

BUT SOMEHOW, SHE FELT DISSATISFIED WITH HER FATE

FETCH THE FOOD BASKET MEENA

LUNCH TIME AT LAST········· SO HUNGRY !!!

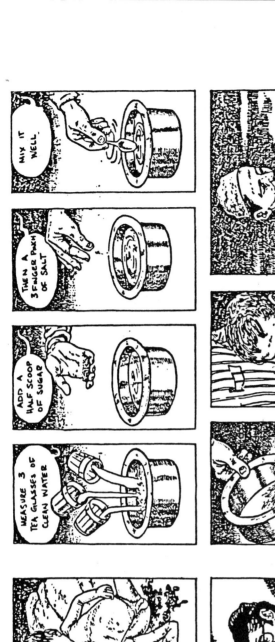

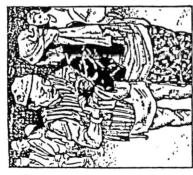